Original title:

Where the Moss Grows

Copyright © 2025 Creative Arts Management OÜ

All rights reserved.

Author: Lila Davenport

ISBN HARDBACK: 978-1-80581-723-9

ISBN PAPERBACK: 978-1-80581-250-0

ISBN EBOOK: 978-1-80581-723-9

Cradle of the Ancient Ones

In the old woods, a snore resounds,
Trees gossip softly, without any bounds.
An owl wears spectacles, wise and round,
While squirrels trade jokes, their laugh quite profound.

Beneath leafy hats, the rabbits will dance,
Springing with joy, they take every chance.
With mushrooms as drums, they start a romance,
Nature's odd circus, a whimsical prance.

The Gentle Touch of Nature's Hand

The brook giggles softly as it flows,
Tickling the fish and slicking their toes.
A frog in a tie croaks business proposals,
While daisies debate the latest 'rose-is rose-als'.

The breeze plays the harp in the rustling trees,
Bees join the band, buzzing melodies.
They're singing of flowers, of sun, and of glee,
While worms in the soil attend with great ease.

Shadows in the Softness

In shadows that dance, a fox spins a tale,
About a lost shoe, a bird's epic fail.
A snail hosts a race, oh, what a grand scale,
Each spectator chuckles, the slowest prevail.

Camouflaged frogs wear the best fashion trends,
With lily pads as hats, they've got lots of fans.
The fireflies flicker, lighting night's ends,
Nature's own nightclub, where laughter extends.

Tales Told in Ferns

Ferns whisper secrets, they giggle and sway,
Telling of mischief that happened today.
A mouse with a mustache leads in the fray,
While the crickets cheer on with their chirpy ballet.

A hedgehog in glasses reads stories from roots,
Of knights with no armor and singing toots.
The laughter erupts from all fluffy brutes,
It's a forest of humor in leafy pursuits.

Lichens and Legends

In a forest where legends play,
Lichens dance on a bright display,
They whisper tales of yesteryears,
While squirrels conspire, plotting their cheers.

Mossy beds for the weary fox,
And rabbits play in polka-dot frocks,
They giggle and hop, avoid the old owl,
Who's snoozing away with a soft, sleepy growl.

A Tincture of Tranquility

Under green canopies, laughter so bright,
A frog sings opera, a curious sight,
With crickets tapping a cheerful refrain,
While the sun drips gold, like sweet candy rain.

A turtle holds court with a snail on the side,
Trading tall tales that stretch quite wide,
Their laughter echoes like bubbles in air,
As the hiccups of nature crackle everywhere.

Reveries in Softened Surroundings

In a world where the soft green lays,
Mice throw parties on sunlit rays,
With cakes made of acorns, a feast to behold,
As dandelions shimmer, their stories retold.

The bees paint pictures while buzzing with glee,
A raccoon plays chess, it's a sight to see,
With pawns made of pebbles, a crafty design,
As laughter erupts in this woodland divine.

When Silence Takes Root

In the quiet nooks where whispers dwell,
The ants plan banquets, oh what a swell!
With crumbs of cheese as their grand delight,
They dance on the logs, what a whimsical sight.

Butterflies gossip with bees on the wing,
Discussing the latest in floral bling,
While a sleepy toad keeps a watchful creep,
Stifling laughter, he's quite hard to keep.

Nature's Quiet Tapestry

In the woods, the squirrels chatter,
As they plan how to steal your platter.
Mushrooms dance in a jolly line,
Whispering secrets over a glass of wine.

The frogs croak out a silly tune,
While bees buzz by, wearing hats like a loon.
The flowers giggle, swaying with grace,
As the trees join in, a leafy embrace.

But the ants march on, all in a row,
Thinking they're part of a wild show.
They laugh with glee as they carry their bread,
While sneaky raccoons plot tricks ahead.

Each path leads to a raucous surprise,
With rabbits in tights and painted ties.
Nature's stage is a comical sight,
Where every creature claims their right!

Beneath the Emerald Shadows

Beneath the ferns, the lizards dance,
Wearing sunglasses, oh what a chance!
The owls hold meetings to gossip around,
While the crickets provide the sound.

The beetles all wear their finest bling,
As the pine cones shout, "Let's do our thing!"
A parade of mice struts and preens,
While bumblebees burst into scenes.

Silly shadows play tag with the sun,
While chipmunks race, thinking it's fun.
A tortoise named Toby runs at a crawl,
While the wind just chuckles, not worried at all.

The mushrooms giggle, wearing their caps,
As rabbits play hopscotch in small grassy gaps.
Nature's humor, found every day,
In the thickets and groves where laughter makes play!

The Serenity of Silenced Footfalls

In the hush of the forest, feet make no sound,
As squirrels discuss who's the best tree around.
The shadows creak and stretch with delight,
As a party of critters get ready for night.

The fireflies twinkle, lighting the way,
While a wise old owl begins to play.
With a wink and a hoot, there's much to explore,
As raccoons pop out, shouting, "Let's have some more!"

Beneath the cloak of mossy green,
The laughter of nature is vividly seen.
They snicker and chuckle in perfect disguise,
While one clumsy deer aptly tries to rise.

Yet, everyone knows that the fun's not complete,
Until the hedgehogs dance on tiny feet.
With a jig and a twist, they prance about,
Inviting the world to join in the shout!

Amongst the Living Tapestry

Among the leaves, there's mischief galore,
As rabbits devise a plan to explore.
The hedges hide tales of giggles and grins,
While snails take bets on who finally wins.

The toads play cards under the old oak,
With hints of lettuce and a pinch of smoke.
A conga line forms, led by a fox,
Wobbling along in mismatched socks!

The gophers hold a race, slow and steady,
While weasels keep score, all warm and ready.
A parade of plants sways to the beat,
As songbirds join in, dancing on their feet.

Each moment a joy, each sound a delight,
With nature's fine humor beneath the moonlight.
Amidst living threads, laughter unfolds,
In every nook, a secret it holds!

Life in the Porous Palate

In the land of crumbly cheese,
Funny tastes make us all freeze.
Pickled dreams dancing with glee,
Who knew salad could sing a spree?

Jellybeans jump on the plate,
Uninvited but feeling great.
Ketchup confesses its sweet lie,
As mustard watches with a sigh.

The soup hums a jazzy tune,
While bread rolls flirt with the spoon.
Pasta twirls in a warm embrace,
Noodles giggle in their place.

Oh, the flavors like friends unite,
Baking fun by candlelight.
In this feast, we laugh and play,
Each bite brings joy, hip-hip-hooray!

Stories Told in the Underbrush

Beneath the bramble, tales unfold,
Of squirrels plotting, brave and bold.
A rabbit's race turns into a rumble,
With wild tales, they all stumble.

The wise old owl, watchful, sly,
Cracks jokes as the crickets cry.
"Why did the snake cross the lane?
To get to the side that's not so plain!"

Frogs leap in with ribbeting pride,
Each telling of their bubbly ride.
The hedgehog snickers, quills on point,
While the earthworms twist in a joint.

In this thicket, laughter is real,
Nature's jesters spin a wheel.
With every rustle and muted chime,
Stories emerge, one giggle at a time.

Where Softness Meets the Stony Path

On stony roads, a cushion lies,
Each pebble tells a tale that flies.
A fluffy creature stops to chat,
"Why don't socks wear hats? Just a spat!"

Laughter echoes from the stones,
As critters boast with silly tones.
"I can flip-flop, can you trot?"
Bouncing softly, they give it a shot.

Squirrels giggle, skipping the tough,
Spongy moments make them huff.
"Let's roll together, let's have a blast,
Life's too short, let not fun be past!"

Softness winks at rocky pride,
Together, they dance side by side.
With chuckles shared on every path,
Funny musings evoke their wrath.

The Glistening Secrets of the Damp

In the misty realms of a soggy glade,
Secrets sparkle, like jokes well laid.
Mushrooms wiggle, dressed in dew,
Hide-and-seek with a funny crew.

The slugs slide through with slick finesse,
Claiming puddles as their address.
"Don't mind us, we'll eat your shoe,
It may taste better than a veggie stew!"

Caterpillars dream in grooves so fine,
Who would've thought they'd dine on shine?
Each little laugh bubbles like spring,
In the damp, every creature can sing.

As droplets gather and giggles bloom,
In this secret, silvery room,
The damp delights, with smiles abound,
In every corner, joy is found.

The Silence of Sleepy Ground

In a patch where sunlight hides,
A snore from roots, the whole world bides.
Grassy blankets, a lumpy bed,
Worms having dreams, or so it's said.

Pillows made of dampened leaves,
Squirrels spinning tales, oh what a weave!
The ants parade in jaunty style,
While sleepy stones grin all the while.

Turtles surfing through the muck,
With clumsy grace, they seem quite stuck.
A yawn escapes from old tree bark,
Echoes fill the air, oh what a lark!

Beneath the calm, a world does spin,
Of funny things that lurk within.
So hush, dear friend, and sit right down,
In a whisper shared, we wear a crown.

Where Secrets Creep and Crawl

In shadows thick, the whispers tread,
To find a joke, beneath the spread.
A spider's web, it giggles loud,
As tiny feet gather 'round the crowd.

Raccoons in masks, they'd steal a snack,
Sneaking around, with each little crack.
They trip on roots, and tumble well,
Secrets spill out, oh what a swell!

The beetles boast of daily feats,
While chasing ants who claim their seats.
Giggling snails race at a crawl,
Excited cheers from mushrooms small.

In this land of soft decay,
Nature plays tricks, come join the fray.
Underneath the mossy veil,
Silly antics abound, don't fail!

Echoes of Forgotten Footsteps

Once there walked a fox in shoes,
Now just whispers, what a ruse!
Each step a giggle, lost in time,
As ancient trees groan quite in mime.

Mice hold meetings at dusk's bright glow,
Discussing tales of friend and foe.
In a game of hide and squeak,
The giggling grass hides all they seek.

Logs speak softly of lost days,
A raccoon's dance, in silly ways.
With each creak of a weathered limb,
Echoes of laughter rise again, so grim!

As shadows stretch, and evening calls,
Take care, dear friend, as starlight falls.
The ground remembers the jokes we tell,
In whispers shared, all is well.

Beneath the Weight of Green

Underneath the leafy dome,
Frogs croak ballads of their home.
With tiny toads in a hopping trance,
They leap about, and start to dance.

Mushrooms gather for their feast,
A banquet fit for the silliest beast.
In joyful chaos, they munch and grin,
As ladybugs spin tales of win.

Beneath the veil of emerald shade,
A ticklish breeze begins its trade.
It scrapes the ferns and shakes the trees,
Sending giggles into the breeze.

So let us play in the dappled light,
Where laughter lingers, taking flight.
In the weight of green, let's find our cheer,
For nature's jest is always near!

Hiding in the Glimmers of Green

In a world full of mystery, so bright,
A squirrel lost his acorns in delight.
He searched high and low, oh what a scene,
But found them all tucked in a coat of green.

A frog wearing glasses hopped with a grin,
Trying to read from a book made of tin.
Underneath leaves, his words went astray,
'Is it hoppy or floppy?' he'd say with dismay.

The ants had a picnic, a feast of sweet cheese,
But forgot to invite the buzz of the bees.
So in danced the flies, like they were elite,
And the ants all agreed, 'This was a bad cheat!'

In shadows of laughter, the mushrooms awake,
With hats made of jokes that they happily take.
They giggle and chortle under the sun,
Where laughter and nature all blend into fun.

Muffled Murmurs from the Woodland Floor

Down by the stream where the river does sigh,
A turtle was dreaming, oh so spry.
He thought he could fly on a leaf, oh so bold,
Until he slipped back, and that story was told.

The gophers had secrets they'd constantly share,
In tunnels beneath, giggles filled up the air.
'Did you hear about Timmy? He danced on a rock!'
The whole lot erupted like pops from a sock.

A hedgehog once tried to bake with no flare,
His cookie dough rolled all over the square.
With sprinkles and nuts, he made quite a mess,
The forest declared it a culinary stress!

All creatures gathered, their giggles did pour,
For tales from the shadows, sweet tales from the floor.
With snacks made of laughter, they counted to three,
And rolled back home happy, as happy could be!

Whispers Beneath the Canopy

Underneath branches where sunlight plays peek,
A squirrel is plotting, he's sly and quite cheek.
With acorns in pockets, he gathers his friends,
To play tricks on rabbits, where the fun never ends.

A wise owl called out with a voice like a breeze,
'Why do you giggle? Just settle with ease!'
The bunnies just laughed and threw carrots around,
And the owl shook his head, all puzzled and brown.

There's a fox with a scarf who's trying to dance,
But tripping on roots, loses quite the chance.
He twirls and he whirls, but he lands in a pile,
The forest erupts in a collective smile.

And as twilight falls, with a blanket of stars,
The whispers continue, beneath trees and bars.
For in every giggle, and each merry sound,
The joy of the wild is forever unbound.

In the Shade of Ancient Stones

In the shade of rocks where the cool breezes puff,
A tortoise was pondering, 'Is this quite enough?'
He opened a café, with leaves on the side,
Serving lettuce lattes, oh what a wild ride!

A raccoon with shades took a seat by the brook,
Flipping through novels with a curious look.
He ordered a donut, icing dripping with glee,
And muttered, 'I think we are all born to be free!'

Through tall grasses swayed, a party began,
With creatures all joining from each little clan.
The giraffes brought the music, odd tunes on the go,
While crickets played drums—oh the rhythm did flow!

In the shade of old stones, the laughter rang clear,
With every chuckle shared, they all drew near.
For in such a space, over cookies and tales,
The spirit of joy spreads like the softest of gales.

Chronicles of the Silent Grove

In a grove where whispers roam,
A squirrel asked, 'Is that my home?'
The trees just chuckled, roots all tied,
While squirrels danced, with giggles wide.

A rabbit hopped, with ears so spry,
'Is it lunchtime? Oh, my oh my!'
The trees rolled laughter, leaves a-flutter,
Telling tales over nutty butter.

Foxes played poker, quite a sight,
With acorns stacked, oh what a night!
They laughed till dawn, no need for sleep,
As owls hooted, secrets to keep.

In this grove, so fun and free,
We gather round for tea and glee,
With every chuckle, joy does grow,
In a world where mischief flows.

Beneath the Lock of Time

Beneath the clock, the shadows laugh,
As time takes nap, now isn't that daft?
A turtle raced a snail so slow,
They both forgot where they had to go.

The daisies danced in fields of green,
While buzzing bees played hide and seek keen.
A butterfly joined, tripping on air,
In this silly game, not a single care.

The sun popped in, a golden clown,
Tickling the gloom that dared to frown.
With giggles bursting, oh what a day,
Who knew time could dance and play?

In this time-lock without a care,
The laughter echoes, filling the air,
Beneath the clock, we're free to roam,
For every tick brings us back home.

In the Embrace of Nature's Kin

Among the branches, where laughter flies,
Chirping birds tell the silliest lies.
A raccoon winks, with a wink so sly,
"Did you see me steal that pie?"

The flowers giggle, swaying in the breeze,
As bees buzz by, "Hey, can we tease?"
They came together for a grand parade,
In this wild world, where fun won't fade.

A grumpy toad tried to croak a song,
But ended up singing it all wrong.
The rabbits rolled, laughing in delight,
As fireflies danced into the night.

In nature's kin, the joy's alive,
With every chuckle, the spirits thrive.
Embraced by laughter, bright and bold,
In this funny tale, let's all be told.

Secrets Held in Softness

In the glade where softness hides,
The mushrooms giggle, no need for guides.
A hedgehog grinned, with quills all tight,
'Come join the fun, it's quite alright!'

The grass grew tall, tickling toes,
A croaky frog in a fancy pose.
'Let's host a ball!' he said with glee,
While daisies twirled so fancifully.

The moon peeked in with a silvery grin,
As magic spun around, where to begin?
A squirrel in top hat, looking dapper,
Called out for fun amid all the clapper.

In the softness, laughter's the key,
Every secret shared, so wild and free.
With whispers and giggles, the night we'll bask,
In a world of joy, no need to ask.

Whispers Beneath the Canopy

In the woods where squirrels dare,
Nuts are hidden here and there.
The owls whisper, 'Did you see?',
A raccoon stealing tea, oh glee!

Frogs are croaking puns at night,
While fireflies dance, oh what a sight!
A deer trips over mossy rocks,
And giggles echo through the docks.

Beneath the leaves, a party stirs,
With mushrooms in their tiny furs.
They laugh and sing 'til dawn does break,
At dawn, they hide, for goodness' sake!

The trees lean in, they want to know,
What secrets lie in breezes slow?
But all they hear is silly cheer,
As critters dance, both far and near.

Secrets of the Shaded Hollow

In the hollow, shadows play,
Where bunnies hop and dance all day.
A turtle sunbathes, thinking wise,
While ants parade in funny ties.

The hedgehogs roll in leaf confetti,
While talking ferns sing tunes so jetty.
A raccoon juggling acorns wide,
Makes everyone laugh, with pride!

The twigs gossip as breezes blow,
"Who picked the color for that crow?"
While gnats perform a tiny ballet,
Beneath the leaves, they steal the play!

A squirrel, wearing shades, takes a stroll,
Chasing dreams and a fried dough roll.
Underneath those laughing trees,
The fun continues with such ease.

Embrace of the Green Veil

Under the veil, giggles abound,
Where secret parties sometimes are found.
A lizard from a branch shouts, 'Hey!'
While critters laugh and dance in sway.

The mushrooms tease, "Come get your prize!",
As butterflies wear silly ties.
The bees hum chords of their sweet tunes,
While ladybugs play charades with moons.

A wise old tree sits, counting laughs,
While chipmunks scribble funny drafts.
The fireflies burst with shining glee,
As all join in, a jubilee!

A squirrel shouts, "Racoon, take a nap!"
While all the critters share a map.
Of spots to skip and hop in fun,
Every leaf a new day begun!

Hidden Life in the Forest's Cradle

In the cradle of the fragrant pine,
A silly rabbit sips on wine.
With acorns stacked like poker chips,
As laughter spills from woodland lips.

A family of frogs plays leap and bound,
Croaking tales of the silly hound.
Butterflies flit, judging their threads,
While critters collide, bumping their heads!

The brook hums songs of mischief and fun,
As tall ferns dance, they've just begun.
Each shadow hides a giggling beast,
Ready to jump and join the feast!

As evening falls with a wink and sigh,
The starlit sky draws a twinkling eye.
In cozy nooks, all creatures cheer,
For every moment brings them here!

The Comfort of Cloistered Roots

In the shaded nook, a fungus sighs,
A toadstool party beneath the skies.
They dance in circles on their tiny toes,
Inviting all the ants to their grand shows.

With laughter rich, a beetle held a toast,
To the colorful critters, they loved the most.
A snail on a chair, it's quite a sight,
Sipping dew drops, what a pure delight!

While worms in jackets play their own charade,
Doing the worm, in the leafy shade.
They wiggle and giggle, oh what a scene,
In this underground jive, they're the dancing green!

With roots intertwining, a living quilt,
A brigade of fungi, all secrets built.
Exuding whimsy, joy in the dirt,
Forever cozy, this is their concert.

Awakenings in the Green Hearth

The squirrels convene for their morning cheer,
While morning glories stretch, bright and clear.
A raccoon juggles acorns, oh what a feat,
As sunbeams tickle their tiny feet.

Under leafy covers, the critters convene,
Planning their day in a glimmering green.
Frogs argue loudly, who can leap best,
While all the flowers gawk, quite impressed.

In this leafy lounge, mischief fills the air,
As hedgehogs roll by in a curious pair.
A meeting of misfits, under branches so wide,
In this jubilant space, there's nowhere to hide!

With tea brewed from dew, the garden's alive,
As fireflies gather, they dance and they dive.
In a whirlwind of chuckles, the woodland awakens,
Life is a party, with joy never shaken!

The Dreams of Quiet Corners

In a pocket of shade, where whispers dwell,
Ladybugs tell secrets, their stories swell.
With twinkling laughter, they share their dreams,
Of cotton candy clouds and jellybean streams.

A stout little rabbit draws up a chair,
And spins tall tales, with the freshest flair.
While crickets chime in with a rhythmic beat,
Creating a symphony, oh so sweet!

The flowers gossip, rolling their petals,
As snappy young sprouts play hopscotch in meddles.
With funny faces and giggles galore,
In this tranquil corner, they always want more!

Expecting no visitors, they simply chat,
While bees throw confetti and dance in a spat.
So join in the whimsy, let laughter unfold,
In these quiet corners, where wonders are bold.

Nature's Hidden Kingdom

Beneath a big leaf, the council does meet,
Gossipy butterflies shuffle their feet.
A wise old caterpillar shares sage advice,
On the best spots for naps stitched with spice.

A parade of ants struts their new haul,
Declaring boldly, they're having a ball.
A firefly flickers, saying "Light up your dreams!"
In this hidden kingdom, nothing's as it seems.

With a flick of a tail, a fish jumps and laughs,
As the frogs ribbit out their joyful drafts.
In a world of whimsy, no room for gloom,
Every nook and cranny birthplace of bloom!

They all join together, a raucous parade,
Where every young sprout shares its antics displayed.
Nature's a party, where silliness reigns,
In the hidden kingdom, where joy never wanes.

The Gentle Pulse of Green Life

In a quiet nook, where the squirrels play,
There's a carpet of green, leading creatures astray.
Frogs wear tiny hats, pigeons don glasses,
Life's a parade in the soft, squishy grasses.

Ants in a line with a crumb of delight,
Arguing over who gets the biggest bite.
A snail on a mission, its shell full of dreams,
Moves at a pace that's slower than beams.

A ladybug giggles at a beetle nearby,
While a misplaced worm gives a puzzled "Oh my!"
Laughter erupts from the roots of a tree,
Where the fungi dance, oh come join the spree!

When raindrops descend like a tickling kiss,
The plants all cheer, oh, what bliss!
In this green kingdom where spirits can soar,
Nature's joke book is full of encore!

Shadows in the Grove

In the depths of the woods, where the shadows entwine,
A raccoon in pajamas is sipping on brine.
With a wink and a nod, he invites you to stay,
For a tea party held in the light's fading ray.

Mushrooms wear hats and throw parties all night,
While the owls hoot softly, 'Oh what a sight!'
The fireflies flicker, their lanterns aglow,
Making a ballet of luminous flow.

A hedgehog brings snacks, it's a feast of delight,
As the rabbits reveal their dance moves so bright.
You'd think it was a circus with all the razzmatazz,
With each critter jumping, giving applause and pizzazz!

As the moon comes to play in the velvet sky dome,
Every shadow is dancing, no creature alone.
What fun it is here, in this woodland retreat,
Where laughter is boundless, and all share a seat!

Underneath Nature's Embrace

Beneath the great branches, with laughter so wide,
A gopher named Gus wore a rather large tide.
He tripped on a twig, oh the ruckus it made,
As the birds all chuckled, "Now that's how you wade!"

Under canopies thick, the critters convene,
Where the bunnies play tag on a vibrant green scene.
A tortoise named Tilly declared herself fast,
But her friends all just giggled, "That joke'll not last!"

The squirrel's on stilts, doing acrobat tricks,
While a chipmunk complains, "I'm all out of picks!"
In this wacky world, where the sunbeams dance low,
Every creature is gleeful, with no room for woe.

As dusk softly settles, the shadows grow tall,
The hedgehogs lay down for a nighttime sprawl.
A lullaby whirl, nature's sweet sigh,
In this cozy embrace, under the night sky!

Life Wrapped in Verdant Hues

In the shady nook, I slip and slide,
A slippery dance where greens collide.
Frogs laugh as I tumble, oh what a sight,
In the jungle gym of nature, pure delight.

Lichens whisper secrets, old as time,
Telling me tales, oh so sublime.
I bow and say sorry as I trip on a root,
Nature's got jokes, I'm the fool in pursuit.

Dandelions giggle as they sway in the breeze,
While ants march by with expert ease.
Caught in a patch, I play hide and seek,
With a curious squirrel, oh so meek.

Each step I take, the ground squishes deep,
I'm an unwitting jester, but no time for sleep.
With nature's laughter echoing through the trees,
Life's a wild circus, oh yes, pretty please!

In the Hidden Nooks of Nature

In the crook of the branch, a robin snores,
While I search for snacks in nature's drawers.
Mushrooms peek out with cheeky grins,
They giggle and wiggle, oh where to begin?

A hedgehog rolls by, all prickles and fluff,
As I trip on a twig, this path's getting tough.
The ferns wave at me, a leafy parade,
Nature's comedy show, I'm often afraid.

I chased a butterfly, oh what a chase,
But tripped on my shoelace, fell flat on my face!
The flowers all chuckled, quite the display,
While bees mocked my dance, buzzing away.

Yet every slip brings laughter, no doubt,
In these wild corners, joy's all about.
So I laugh with the plants, join their fun spree,
In the hidden nooks, where the wild things be!

A Carpet of Dreams

Lying on the green, I close my eyes tight,
Dreaming of adventures, soaring in flight.
But ants march past, with purpose so grand,
While I'm stuck daydreaming, lost in the sand.

A dragonfly buzzes, talks like my bro,
"You've got to move, stop being so slow!"
But I just grin, as I lounge like a king,
To the moss-covered edges, my praises I sing.

Each leaf is alive, gossiping away,
Telling tall tales of things that won't stay.
A rabbit peeks out, ears all alert,
"Why sit when the world around you is dirt?"

With giggles in bushes and chuckles in blooms,
Nature's a stage with its own funny tunes.
So I roll in the soft, plushy quilt on the ground,
To a symphony of laughter, joy unbound!

Memories in the Moist Earth

Digging in dirt, a child's delight,
Finding old treasures tucked out of sight.
A worm waves hello, drenched in good cheer,
"Come share in my mud, let's make memories here!"

Sunlight peeks in, warming my face,
While grasshoppers giggle, hopping with grace.
Each squishy discovery is met with a grin,
As I'm crowned the king of the muck and the din.

Tadpoles are splashing, a raucous parade,
They flip and they flop; oh what a charade!
I join in their fun, making squelchy sounds,
With nature as my stage, laughter abounds.

So if you're feeling blue and need a good laugh,
Come join this party in the muddy path.
In memories made where the good times churn,
In the moist earth's embrace, it's your turn!

The Unseen World Awaits

Beneath the leafy cover, critters play,
In secret meetings, night and day.
A squirrel in a suit, oh what a sight,
Debating acorns in the fading light.

Worms don their glasses, looking quite wise,
Sharing deep thoughts with very few sighs.
Each pebble a leader, each leaf a friend,
In this quirky world, laughter won't end.

A turtle in sneakers, racing with glee,
Shouts, "I'm the fastest, just wait and see!"
But a slow little snail gives a shrug and grins,
"Just you wait, dear friend; I'll beat you with spins!"

So come take a peek, and giggle a bit,
Join in the fun; don't ever sit.
For in this hidden realm, it's not what it seems,
It's a carnival of joy, bursting with dreams.

Amongst the Greenery's Caress

With tiny fairies having a feast,
A pizza made of leaves—oh, what a beast!
They twirl and spin with a giggly cheer,
Dodging the rays of the sun's bright sphere.

A grasshopper dressed in vibrant flair,
Hosts a dance party without a care.
"Jump this way!" he says with glee,
While ants in tuxedos sip on sweet tea.

A raccoon in heels tries hard to impress,
But trips on a twig, oh what a mess!
Laughter erupts from the crowd so grand,
"Better luck next time, with a steadier hand!"

Among tangled greens and the laughter's glow,
Nature's a stage, where funny antics flow.
With each silly tale and whimsical jest,
The world of the green will give you the best.

In the Shadows of the Giants

Beneath the towering trees, tales unfold,
Of a beetle with dreams, feeling quite bold.
He boasts of his conquests, those mighty falls,
While whispering secrets to boulder-sized walls.

A mouse on a mission, his mission so clear,
Hopes to ride a leaf without any fear.
As it flutters away, he gives a loud shout,
"Hey, wait for me—don't leave me out!"

A clever old owl, perched high up near,
Jokes with the wind, with a raucous cheer.
"Why did the branches break up with the tree?"
"Because they found someone more rooted, you see!"

In this grand theater, beneath the sky's light,
Life's simple humor brings pure delight.
So lift your spirits and join in the jest,
Where nature itself becomes laughter's nest.

Grounded in Green Reveries

A dandelion dreams of being a star,
Sprouting wishes while puffing from afar.
"Blow me, oh friend!" it pleads with a grin,
"Let's see if my hopes can finally begin!"

The ants throw a party; they dance on the line,
With crumbs of old pizza, they happily dine.
A ladybug DJ spins tunes with flair,
While beetles all gather—oh, the joy in the air!

A frog leaps by, in a custom-made hat,
Says, "Catching flies? Well, I'm fine with that!"
He strikes a pose, so suave and spry,
While chuckling at bugs that just pass him by.

In this grounded haven of laughter and cheer,
Life's little moments draw everyone near.
So whisper your wishes to the green so vast,
And let those giggles bring joy unsurpassed.

In the Heart of the Woodland Whisper

In the woods, the squirrels play,
Chasing shadows through the day.
With acorns flying all around,
Who knew chaos could be found?

The owls are hooting jokes at night,
While bats laugh, wings taking flight.
A deer trips on a hidden root,
That's nature's slapstick, oh so cute!

The trees gossip, swaying 'round,
While tiny fairies tumble down.
They giggle loud, with twinkling eyes,
Creating mischief, oh how time flies!

Each creature shares a silly tale,
Of dizzy dives and frantic flail.
In this wild, whimsical abode,
Life's a riot on this winding road!

A Symphony of Stillness

In the shadow of the tall pine,
A frog croaks out a silly line.
The crickets' orchestra plays a tune,
While hare explores the woodland moon.

The stillness hums with laughter's song,
As flowers giggle all day long.
The breeze tickles leaves with delight,
Nature's chuckle fills the night.

A snail drags on at a snail's pace,
While breezy whispers quicken the race.
"Excuse me, pardon!" the cobweb sighs,
As a wandering ant nearly flies!

In this calm, the whimsy grows,
A tapestry of funny prose.
From bark to bloom, it's clear to see,
Nature's got a sense of glee!

Nature's Secret Harvest

Beneath the ferns, a treasure lies,
A rogue potato with bright blue eyes.
It winks at me, a cunning thief,
Rolling downhill, oh what a grief!

Mushrooms dance in spots so bright,
While ants march in a jolly fight.
"Oh, look at me!" the dandelion beams,
"I'm the queen of all wild dreams!"

Ladybugs play hide-and-seek,
While whiskered cats sneak up to peek.
Each moment holds a playful prize,
Nature's joke in every guise!

The harvest of laughter fills the air,
Every squabble and secret pair.
In this garden of cheerful grins,
Nature whispers where the fun begins!

Alive in Lush Abandon

In a meadow bursting bright,
Bunnies bounce with pure delight.
They dance and skip like silly fools,
In the shade of leafy stools.

A chubby fox rolls down the hill,
Belly up, what a crazy thrill!
The ladybugs join in the spree,
A polka party under the tree!

Wildflowers sway, a colorful sight,
While the wind nudges them in delight.
A bumblebee attempts a dance,
But tumbles down with a sideway glance!

Life's a circus in nature's land,
With a laugh that's truly grand.
Each moment bursts with playful cheer,
In this lush retreat, we hold dear!

A Lush Lullaby

In a forest of giggles and soft moss,
I found a frog wearing my old shoe.
He croaked me a tune, quite dapper and boss,
As he hopped with a grin—what a quirky view!

The squirrels were dancing, a cha-cha in style,
They tried on my hat, now it fits like a glove.
With acorns as drums, they played all the while,
And I joined in the fun, feeling sparkles of love!

A rabbit with shades said, 'Why not take a seat?'
He offered me carrots, assorted in hue.
His dance moves were wild, full of rhythm and beat,
We danced through the grass, tipping hats to the dew!

So if you think nature is quiet and meek,
Just wander a bit, let surprises unfold.
With each little creature, there's laughter to seek,
And joy in the small things that never get old!

Treading on Soft Earth

I slipped on a mushroom, it squished like a pie,
The ants all applauded, they brought me a cheer.
'Come join our parade!' they all shouted, 'Oh my!'
With ants in top hats, we marched without fear!

A hedgehog named Bob started juggling just then,
With apples and berries, he twirled with a skirmish.
The more that he wobble, the funnier, when
He plopped in a puddle—oh, what a sweet flourish!

We climbed on a log that rolled like a ride,
But oh, how it flipped, we tumbled and tumbled.
Then giggles erupted, we laughed side by side,
In the softest of earth where we finally grumbled.

So next time you wander through nature's delight,
Just watch for the creatures and their silly fun.
For laughter and joy are all tucked in tight,
In each squishy step, as we dance in the sun!

A Journey Through Nature's Veils

Beneath leafy curtains, I tripped on a root,
A squirrel in pajamas was sipping his tea.
He winked as he pointed to magical fruit,
Said, 'Eat this, my friend, you'll sprout wings like me!'

The wayward breeze brought a giggling gust,
It tickled my nose, made me snort like a pig.
I laughed as it twirled through the greenish dust,
And a fox in a top hat did a comical jig!

I wandered through fog that was swirling with cheer,
A mushroom convention was set deep in shade.
Each fungus was shrieking with laughter, oh dear!
I ventured to join in their wild masquerade.

So dance through the veils, let your worries disperse,
Nature's a stage for the strange and the fun.
In every nook, you'll find humorous verse,
So grab that odd fruit and let giggles outrun!

Encounters with the Unseen

In the spin of a tale, I met a sprite,
He juggled with fireflies and danced with the dew.
He asked me for cookies—what a silly sight!
I answered with laughter, 'I've baked just for you!'

The trees whispered secrets, a tickle of glee,
As shadows threw parties with mushrooms galore.
A badger with shades shouted, 'Look, it's me!'
He moonwalked right past, making everyone roar!

I spotted a doorway, a portal of green,
It zoomed with a zap, taking me for a ride.
To a land full of giggles, oh what a scene!
With clouds made of candy and rivers of pride!

So step into places where laughter resides,
There's magic in moments that somehow seem lost.
With sprites and laughter, where the joy often hides,
You'll find that the unseen can be quite the cost!

Fabric of the Forgotten Wild

In a forest so lush, the trees hold their breath,
Whispers of secrets in the dance of their deaths.
Squirrels in suits throw a grand masquerade,
While branches are gossiping, shade is their trade.

Mushrooms, like Londoners, gossip away,
Fungus and ferns in a sprightly ballet.
A rabbit with spectacles reads poetry loud,
As the daisies all chuckle, forming a crowd.

Old owls roll their eyes at the jokes of the day,
While bees play the harp in their haphazard way.
The crickets provide a raucous delight,
As nature's odd symphony echoes the night.

Through branches and brambles, the mischief unfolds,
In this forgotten wild, hilarity holds.
A dance of the weird, a laugh in the breeze,
In the fabric of nature, it's all meant to please.

Patches of Poetry in the Shade

Beneath leafy blankets, the critters convene,
A gathering splendid, a woodland scene.
Frogs recite sonnets with great pomp and flair,
As butterflies judge them from high in the air.

Squirrels in tutus are prancing about,
While hedgehogs recite verses, trying to shout.
The trees shake their leaves, a grand audience true,
In patches of shade where wild laughter grew.

A dandelion dreamer lost in her thought,
Wonders why daisies are always distraught.
With giggles and grins, they share all their fears,
In this patchwork of poetics, the joy simply cheers.

When night falls, the crickets compose a new tune,
While owls nod approvingly, wink at the moon.
In patches of poetry, let the laughter blend,
For nature's own humor will always transcend.

The Green Embrace of a Lost World

In a realm of the green, where odd critters play,
Frogs wearing crowns cheer for the sun's grand ballet.
The trees clap their hands, though they do not have palms,

While insects compose their delightful psalms.

A fox in a cape plots a heist of the cheese,
While snails form a conga line, just to please.
With mushrooms as judges and toads on the stand,
The trial of the silly is truly quite grand.

The flowers all giggle as sunlight cascades,
Knowing fairies mix colors with sweet serenades.
In this lost world, where the oddities thrive,
Humor and nature are joyfully alive.

When evening descends, the antics won't cease,
With shadows that chuckle and light that won't lease.
In the green embrace of a vibrant delight,
The spirits of laughter dance into the night.

Where Nature's Fingers Trace

In a giggling glade, where the sunlight likes to play,
Ladybugs host parties that last through the day.
Mice in tuxedos serve cheese on a tray,
While ferns twirl around in their emerald ballet.

The pond has its mirror, reflecting the show,
As turtles in top hats say, "Hey, just go slow!"
A marvel, a riddle, this chaos of cheer,
Where nature's own fingers scribble fun, my dear.

The ants stage a play about lost laundry tales,
While cricket musicians strum joy on their scales.
Dancing through daisies, this lively parade,
Where laughter and whimsy in sunshine cascade.

As twilight creeps near, the revelry slows,
Yet the echoes of laughter, like wind, gently blows.
In nature's warm arms, so free and so wide,
The smiles of the woodland shall never subside.

Shadows on the Softened Stone

In a garden of giggles, I trip and I sway,
With shadows that dance on a bright sunny day.
You'd think I'm a master, a ballet on ground,
But my shoes have their plans, and I'm falling around.

The rocks play their tricks, they chuckle and tease,
As I fumble like jelly, oh please, oh please!
A tumble, a trip, then a soft little laugh,
A dance with the shadows, my unique autograph.

I compete with the critters, oh what a delight,
A wiggle, a jiggle in the warm morning light.
They scurry away, made of feathers and fluff,
While I'm checking my shoelaces—this is really tough!

So here's to the stones, and their mirrored stare,
They watch as I wiggle, with a slip and a flare.
In shadows and giggles, I continue to roam,
As long as I'm laughing, I'm still right at home.

Beneath the Blushing Ferns

Beneath leafy blankets that swish and they swoon,
I peek at the critters, they're holding a tune.
The ferns have a rhythm, a rustle and sway,
I join in their jiggle; it's a mossy ballet!

A snail slowly slides on her slick little shell,
While I bounce like a rabbit, and nearly fell.
She laughs with a wink, as I hop to her beat,
In this verdant charade, like it's all on repeat.

The ferns are my comrades; they blush and they giggle,
As I trip over roots that just love a good wiggle.
With every experience, a new twist and turn,
I cherish each moment; oh, what will I learn?

So if you're feeling fussy or stuck in a rut,
Just follow the ferns, let laughter uncut.
With friends made of fronds and a snail on my feet,
We frolic and tumble, now isn't that sweet?

The Quiet Watch of the Old Trees

Old trees speak in whispers, while I do a dance,
With limbs that are creaking, they take a chance.
I wiggle and jiggle, as they look on with pride,
While vines curl around, saying, 'Come take a ride!'

They chuckle in breezes, with leaves fluttering free,
As I trip over roots, oh, what a sight to see!
A wobble and tumble, then I wave my arms wide,
Pretending it's flair, not just lack of my stride.

The squirrels are snickering, they scurry in glee,
I'm quite the performance, a dance comedy.
But old sturdy witnesses in their leafy crowns,
They wink and they nod at my slapstick renowns.

So I thank these wise elders, with their mossy embrace,
For sharing their laughter, it has its own grace.
As I shuffle and fumble, embracing the falls,
I find joy in the journey, where nature enthralls.

Soft Footfalls on Ancient Ground

With soft little footfalls, I wander once more,
On ancient soil that has stories galore.
Each step is a giggle, a bounce in delight,
As I trip over secrets hidden from sight.

The earth holds its laughter in cracks and in crumbs,
While I shuffle along, dancing over the hums.
The stones wink at me, 'Come play with your fate!'
In this ballet of blunders, it's never too late.

There's a chuckle in pebbles and a tickle in trees,
As I twirl and I stumble with whimsical ease.
The past pops up laughing in each gentle fall,
And I'm sharing the stage with the moss-covered call.

Through the cracks in the ground, and the whispers above,

I find joy in each misstep, a strange kind of love.
With soft footfalls ringing in this playful parade,
I flourish in folly, where the fun never fades.

Between the Roots and Rocks

A squirrel once danced on a stone,
He thought all the world was his throne.
But tripped on a root,
Now he's shaking his boot,
And grumbling about how he's alone.

The beetles all giggled, a crowd,
As the chipmunk just pouted out loud.
"You call that a fall?"
He tried to stand tall,
But slipped in the mud like a cowd.

The old log just snickered with glee,
Said, "Life's like a game, wait and see."
The branches all sway,
In their own silly way,
As laughter resounds through the tree.

So next time you wander the grove,
Just remember what creatures behove.
With roots and with rocks,
And silly old socks,
It's a riot where nature's in love.

Beneath the Whispering Pines

A hedgehog named Benny, quite spry,
Wore a hat that was very nearby.
It blew off one day,
He chased it away,
And bumped into a grumpy old fly.

The pines chuckled softly above,
As Benny just couldn't get enough.
He rolled in the dirt,
With a wild, goofy flirt,
And thought that the fly would just love.

A rabbit looked on, filled with cheer,
"Hey, Benny, come join us right here!"
But Benny was stuck,
In a puddle of muck,
And all he could do was just leer.

At dusk when the shadows would cower,
Benny finally stood up with power.
He danced in the glade,
In the twilight parade,
While the pines wished him one final hour.

Nature's Quiet Sanctuary

A turtle named Larry was slow,
He trudged through the flowers' soft glow.
With a snack in his shell,
He'd whistle quite well,
While dreaming of far-off places to go.

A raucous crow cawed from a high stake,
"Hey, slowpoke, you're just a mistake!"
Larry looked up high,
With a wink in his eye,
"And you're just a noisy heartache!"

Amidst all the foliage thick and lush,
They shared in a moment, a hush.
With laughter they found,
In their hearts they were bound,
As nature waved at them, quiet and plush.

So Larry just grinned at the crow,
"Life's a dance, don't you see? Just let go!"
The crow flapped and glared,
But together they dared,
To laugh as the gentle winds blow.

In the Embrace of the Old Ones

A wise owl sat snug in his tree,
Pondering life's sweet mystery.
He'd tell silly tales,
Of fish in the gales,
And sing to the moon for some tea.

The raccoons gathered round with delight,
Their masks gleamed so bright in the night.
They'd throw in a joke,
And the owl's eyes would poke,
As laughter soared high, oh what sight!

"Why did the frog cross the big stream?"
The owl hooted loud, "What a dream!"
"To leap for a vote,
On the dress of a goat!"
Now that was a funny old theme.

So under the gaze of the stars,
They shared tales of ducks with guitars.
With giggles and fun,
'Til the rise of the sun,
They felt like the moon and the jars.

Encounters in the Depths

In a swampy land, I tripped on a frog,
He winked at me, a slimy little rogue.
I asked for a dance, he croaked with delight,
But slipped right away, oh, what a sight!

A turtle passed by, wearing a hat,
It claimed to be fast, imagine that!
I challenged him to a race by the bank,
He smiled, but sat down, filling my prank.

The dragonflies buzzed with a comic sting,
As I chased shadows, they flapped their wing.
One veered so close, I thought I could grab,
Just for a laugh, oh, what a blab!

Then a snail slid in, said, "Hey, hold on tight!
I'm the speedy one here, let's race with all might!"
I laughed at his joke, the slowest of all,
But he slid on by, and I started to fall.

Calm Amidst the Verdant

Beneath green canopies, I found my place,
With squirrels entertaining, in a frantic chase.
One paused to chat, with a nut in his maw,
And claimed he could juggle, I laughed at the flaw.

The ferns waved gently, giving a cheer,
As I settled in coolness, free of all fear.
A bumblebee buzzed, wearing spectacles neat,
Said, "I'm a scholar, my studies are sweet!"

A wise old owl hooted jokes from the trees,
His timing impeccable, brought me to knees.
"Why did the raccoon cross the marshy bog?
To steal all the biscuits from that silly dog!"

I chuckled so hard, I nearly fell down,
As frogs shared tales, they wore pranks like a crown.
Joy echoed loudly among all the shrugs,
In this lovely place, where laughter just hugs.

The Poetry of Lost Paths

I wandered the woods without any map,
Followed a bird singing, oh what a trap!
It led me in circles, a clumsy ballet,
But I laughed all the while, lost in the fray.

A mischievous fox poked his head from behind,
With a wink and a grin, said, "You're one of a kind!"
I offered him snacks, all the crumbs in my sack,
He turned up his nose, "I'll stick to my snack!"

A hedgehog appeared, all spines and all sass,
"Let's build a monopoly of grass, if you please!"
And so we conspired, a strangest of teams,
In the bustling woods, among giggles and dreams.

With twigs for our pencils, we crafted profound,
The poetry of paths, where lost is the sound.
And on every corner, a heckle or two,
Ever grateful for the woods' playful view.

Refuge of the Resting Breath

Upon a soft patch where the earth felt alive,
I found a cool spot where all critters thrive.
The lizards were lounging, pensively serene,
As I gently tiptoed, not wanting to be seen.

A chubby raccoon grinned, his belly so round,
Told tales of treasure he cached underground.
"I've got cookies and gold, but don't tell a soul,
You're welcome to visit; just don't steal my roll!"

With giggles galore, I took a deep breath,
In my leafy retreat, I felt far from death.
A chorus of crickets joined in for the show,
In this refuge of bliss, how the good vibes flow!

As twilight descended, shadows grew long,
I hummed to the crickets, felt like I belonged.
And with no plans at all, just chilling at ease,
I embraced every moment, with giggles and trees.

Echoes of the Silent Grove

In the woods, a squirrel sings,
About its stash and nutty bling.
Trees sway, they cannot hold back,
Laughter echoes, on this track.

A rabbit dons a top hat bold,
As if for tea with friends of old.
He hops about with great delight,
In this forest, what a sight!

The owl pretends to read a book,
While all the mice just stop and look.
With tiny glasses perched, they cheer,
"Who knew we'd find a scholar here?"

And in the shade, a bear in pants,
Dances clumsily, can't take a chance.
His two left feet, they steal the show,
In this whimsical grove, let's go!

Lush Layers of Forgotten Earth

Beneath the leaves, a secret lies,
A party with ants in tiny ties.
They waltz in circles, so refined,
In their world, it's all perfectly aligned.

A worm in shades greets the sun,
"Hey there, friend! Let's have some fun!"
They dig and giggle, what a scene,
On this layer of soft, green sheen.

Bright mushrooms wear the funniest hats,
While snails debate about the bats.
"Do they sleep in caves, or climb the trees?"
Giggles echo, carried by the breeze.

Toadstools join in, a merry crew,
Juggling raindrops, oh, what a view!
Nature's circus, full of glee,
Come dance beneath the old oak tree!

The Tapestry of Time and Green

In the tapestry of tangled vines,
A frog croaks out his best punchlines.
He's got the jokes, he's full of cheer,
Making sure that all can hear.

A butterfly, in colors bright,
Flies in to join the funny flight.
"I hope you laugh, it's time to jest,
Fly with me, we'll be the best!"

A spider weaves a web with flair,
Catching flies, he's a master of air.
"What do you think? Is it a skill?"
As laughter echoes, it's quite the thrill!

The trees listen in, with boughs that sway,
They share their tales at the end of the day.
This lively realm, with joy it's rife,
In the fabric of nature, we laugh at life!

Beneath a Blanket of Nature's Quilt

Under covers of twinkling leaves,
A hedgehog rolls where all believes.
"Are you my pillow? Are you my bed?"
He snorts and snores, then turns his head.

Fluffy clouds dance in a gentle breeze,
While grasshoppers play on their knees.
"Hop over here, the game is on!"
They leap around till the light is gone.

A curious raccoon peeks with glee,
"Did you hear the one about the tree?"
"Oh, please!" cries out a busy bee,
"Tell it quick, won't you, to me!"

This cozy quilt of nature's thread,
Holds laughter and joy, where dreams are fed.
In patches of green, where tales unfold,
Life's a laughter, a happiness told!

A Haven of Green Beneath

Beneath the trees, the shadows play,
A carpet soft, where critters sway.
A squirrel dances, his acorn prize,
While I trip over roots, to my surprise.

The ants hold meetings under the sun,
Discussing lunch that's just begun.
A rabbit sneezes, then laughs with glee,
As I step in mud, so clumsily.

Beneath the ferns, life does not cease,
It's like a party, one big tease.
I sit and wonder, how can this be?
Nature's fun, and I'm the key!

So take a seat on ground so sweet,
With bugs and laughter, it's quite a treat.
Join the ruckus, feel the cheer,
In this green haven, joy is near.

The Subtle Art of Stillness

On a log that's gone to sleep,
I find myself with secrets to keep.
A frog attempts his finest croak,
But out he jumps—what a joke!

The world around is calm, so still,
Yet squirrels race with endless thrill.
I sip my tea, and hear the cheer,
Of nature's laughter, loud and clear.

Mushrooms pop up, they're having fun,
A tiny dance beneath the sun.
The slowest sloth gives a wink my way,
"Chill out, friend, it's a lazy day!"

So here I sit, where quiet reigns,
With all the joy that stillness contains.
Nature's giggles all around,
In calmness, oh, such mirth is found!

Dreaming in Softness

In a world where soft things lie,
Dreams are woven under the sky.
A caterpillar dons a tiny hat,
While the grass giggles—imagine that!

Pillows of moss, so warm and nice,
Invite the ants for afternoon spice.
They dance and twirl, then freeze, oh dear,
As I chuckle, they can't see me here!

Dandelions whisper sweet nothings low,
The clouds above in fluffy throw.
A butterfly's having a fit,
Because it can't find where to sit.

So lay me down on the gentle ground,
In this soft world, true peace is found.
With laughter shared between the blades,
In dreams of softness, joy cascades!

In Thickets of Tender Growth

In a thicket where nature's bright,
A snail claims royal, slow delight.
While lilies giggle, frogs all croak,
As branches sway in silent joke.

The bushes rustle, gossip in bloom,
While bees buzz by, a sweet perfume.
I try to walk, but trip on air,
And fall into a furry bear!

The rabbits chuckle as I roll,
In this soft mess, I've lost control.
A thicket party, who knew the fun?
Nature's pranksters, always on the run!

So when you venture, take a glance,
In thickets thick, join the dance!
For laughter hides where green things grow,
A world of joy, we'll always know!

Hushed Harmonies of the Understory

In the shady glade where secrets lie,
The squirrels hold court, they laugh and sigh.
With tiny top hats and tails all a-swish,
They discuss acorns, their gourmet dish.

Frogs in bow ties croak songs of delight,
While slugs groove along, glistening bright.
A beetle struts by with a swagger so bold,
While twirling his partner, a leaf, we are told.

With ferns as the curtains and daisies the stage,
The critters perform, their wild antics engage.
A melody found in the rustle of leaves,
Brings forth laughter from all who believe.

While onlookers giggle from shadows nearby,
They throw popcorn, not caring who'll fly.
In this woodland show, nothing's too silly,
For nature's a jester, both sweet and frilly.

The Breath of Verdant Dreams

In the land of the green, where the ferns do flaunt,
A bird sings a tune, with a very short rant.
He claims he's the king, with a crown made of grass,
But everyone knows he can't quite hold sass!

The turtles play poker with leaves as their chips,
While hedgehogs sip tea, taking dainty sips.
A dandelion fluffs, spreading wishes so wide,
As the garden gnomes dance, they can't help but glide.

Bumblebees buzz with a wiggly jig,
While ants in tuxedos are rather bigwig.
In dreams made of emerald, all creatures convene,
A festival blooms, oh, what a funny scene!

Amidst all the laughter, a wise old oak smirks,
As the vines weave tales of their gossiping quirks.
With wind as their friend, they shuffle and sway,
In this merry kingdom, let's laugh all day!

Gentle Currents of Time

A river of giggles flows swift and free,
With stones that wear hats and sport quite the spree.
Fish tell tall tales, with a splash and a blink,
While turtles debate about how much to drink!

The rocks have opinions on fashionable trends,
While frogs croak their thoughts, as they make amends.
They claim that the tide is just laughter set loose,
In this watery world, it's all a big ruse!

The willows tell stories in whispers so sweet,
Of old camping trips where they baked fish to eat.
But who could believe such bizarre little fables?
As moths flutter by, wearing coats of lace tables.

With splashes and smiles, they dance through the light,
Crafting ripples that shimmer, pure joy in their flight.
In waters so warm, a giggle can sway,
And the moon watches closely, laughing at play.

The Heartbeat of a Hidden Realm

In a nook of the woods, where shadows conspire,
A raccoon in jammies dreams by the fire.
His whiskers are twitching, he's plotting a feast,
With pastry delights to gather the beast!

There's a party tonight, under stars that will wink,
With owls as the bouncers, don't you dare stink!
The rabbits are dressed in their fanciest wear,
While crickets play tunes, filling up the air.

A hedgehog reveals he's a master chef,
With acorns and herbs, he's a playful elf.
They toast with their cups made of mushroom caps,
And giggle as secrets escape through their laps.

With fireflies lighting the pathways so bright,
The woodland's alive with laughter and light.
A heartbeat that echoes in every branch and seam,
Tales told in the night, all born from a dream.

www.ingramcontent.com/pod-product-compliance
Lightning Source LLC
Chambersburg PA
CBHW072130070526
44585CB00016B/1610